PASSAGES

By

Evan A Jordan

For K

Contents

The Steps of Grand Central Station

I've fallen for this before
Back when New York was so cool
Even the pigeons were assholes
And the upper-classes made portraits
Of themselves and their children
Like paparazzi, hiding out in bathrooms
Peeking from behind flaming bushes
When children owned propeller planes
Spider Monkeys were common house pets
Alien Filipino and Latino nannies lined
The Upper West like a massive reef
Healthy with a population of feeder fish
Jazz played in elevators and night watchmen's
Black eyes and pressed slacks shone, a coffee
And a cigarette could be partook anywhere
You pleased, sidewalks so clean you could change
A baby in their reflection, now bankruptcy is
The golden mean, the standard, like a bald
Eagle with popcorn chicken in his beak
Grand Central so thick with flashes
You can barely see the night through white
The constellations gone, disappeared in glare

Szczecin-Krakow, Poland

The years start to float between us
Like tapioca balls suspended in bubble tea
News comes of your recent acquisition
By an important gallery in SoHo, an Eritrean
Roasts nuts, giving off a Christmas whiff
Reaches out a hand like an unleavened loaf
Cringe away from the curb, shy from the subtle
Traffic of eye contact, revert from the memory
To the kitchen with black coffee and the purring
How you could shift your ribs, not hips, not
The tapestry hang of frail Japanese shoulders
The punch of bones, a taut fist above Argentine hips
Your nationality and mine, everything was elsewhere
Shallow perception, our bodies embedded in the prescriptive
Stories we were told during summer dug up roots, hacked away
At the tree of past, a single branch, snapped free
On the overnight train from Szczecin, smoke
Filled passageways clamped with vodka breath
The mutterings of many men, finally *macht frei*
Escaped from the eternal tour guide, took off headphones
Aimless through sun like an ironing board, read plaques
Of names, so many Putzes and Roses, snapshots framed

Various Electricities

What happens when rain
Starts clicking in the night
And various electricities
Come firing through sinuses
Open up a blast hole
Of adrenaline
In the lungs and eyes
Of every child
Lying awake in bed
Window open to the breeze
And the ions charged like jumper cables
Of dreams ignited like spark plugs
Crackling through synapses on the sound
Waves of seven count thunder

Metro Insurgentes, Distrito Federale

Where all the world gets lost
At the *Entrada* to the great below
Forty cops in riot gear at 5AM

A kid born in the 90s, punk
Rocking like its 1985 again — when
This eternal city tried to swallow itself

Whole — his heroin bride, 14 years old
Torn jeans, too big hoodie, candy red
Lipstick smeared on like semen, she waits

The metro rumbles up from below, spits out
A fresh crop of customers, a hundred men
On haunches wait, to polish boots, become

Mirrors, a lithe gay couple kissing, spines
Arched like this late night parting could be
Their lips final meeting beneath darkness

Grace Avenue, Toronto

During Fall I like to sit by myself on a bench
In the park across the street where fog hides
In the valley beneath Harbord Street leaves
Begin to drop easily with immeasurable grace
My headphones on and hood up, the volume
Turned low enough to hear the wind. I watch
As the squirrels furtively gather their acorns
Some are aggressive, hoarders already gaining
Weight. I like to listen to bands that are almost
Forgotten, were never quite great, on repeat, Whatever
By the Butthole Surfers, maybe a bit of Creed. Quietly
The small animals collect their stores for winter, hide
Their inner life - why some must inevitably want sex more
Than nuts. Others probably don't give a fuck about their
Babies: eat them alive, or simply neglect their tiny, bald
Offspring. Why is it that only some squirrels choose
To gorge? Dreaming every night of acorns and the long
Lonely months of sleep. What about the squirrel that dreads
Waking? A new day in the park, endless seasons of green
Unable to stick around for the cold winter gloom, the poor
Squirrel has to imagine the possibility of snow buried beneath
Whiteness in the cranny of a maple tree, longing for
Walks by the sea in that other world south of the freeway
I refuse to believe my thoughts are more relevant than this
Vagrant rodent considering a mad dash in front of a Mercedes
Roaring over the cracked pavement way up above me
On Grace Avenue

Reading Breakfast at Tiffany's

The dirt smell of strong coffee before it's cut with milk. Pain
From a lanced boil. The face of an anguished lover making
An omelette. Unlit cigarettes on the sill. The underside of
An elbow with eczema. Leonard Cohen. Essays on literature
By women who subtly stifle gasps while they read on
The subway. The idea that Carver and Cheever lived
Somewhere as flat and drab as Iowa. Pong and Donkey Kong.
The first time your blood was drawn. David Bowie
In The Labyrinth. Leyendo Borges en español. Not apologizing
For your blood. Tobermory, Ontario and D.F. Feeling alone and
Not wanting to comprehend the afterwardness of melancholy
And yesterday's weather. Cheap white wine. Hoarse laughter
Under blooming trees after midnight. Coming through
Surgery. The hate only friends who have shared a towel
Can know. The Northern Lights are loud. Mountains
Somewhere in the Sierra Madres eight hours south of Oaxaca
On hallucinogens. A pale stranger's hands palsied and unsure
As they pour a glass of ice water. Knowing it is okay. Aubade
By Philip Larkin. Strawberry Fields Forever. Flora, Fauna.
Lighting a match and inhaling the flame. That metaphors are
All the same. Forgetting the name of someone you just met
Even though you're already planning to propose with a
Skywriter. Hollywood bombs, ice cream and ignoring
Everything. The occasional self-effacing joke regardless of
Your health. Eating shit. Knowing that everything is okay
Even though you are going to die and so is everyone you've
Ever known. Forgetting the big ideas like the moon landing
And theory of relativity, gravity or quantum physics. Calling
Someone out on their truths.

Like a Happy Ending

Campy, buxom stars cheap as a tall can
Of ice cold Labatt Blue
I'm trying too hard, I can already hear
Desperation in these first few lines
Down on my knees, I'm begging you
Please, won't you redact with me

There's nothing plangent about it
This keyboard, the rain outside, the window falling
Like a message in a bottle, I can't fix this script
Nothing to recollect, it's a Monday of ten-cent metaphors
What do we have left to say
To each other, til death do us

I'm eating cold tofu from a Styrofoam container
Drinking a beer at quarter to five, thinking
Maybe this poetry thing will keep the night at bay
Stave off the consolation prize of indigestion
Somewhere over the rainbow
Of cliche and hard-fought sentences

There's a line break that was meant to be you and
Me forever, no doubt it's out there, dancing in the dark
Asking Mayakovsky and O'Hara to a lunch date
Grilled cheese and French fries with a strawberry shake
All that other shit washing away
Out to sea like a simile in the undertow

Domingo en D.F.

All writers desperately want to be
Painters of lovers and landscapes
Frivolous colour and deep-rooted
Hate, breaths of early Spring
The flutter
Of leaves in a fractal
Tight and precarious
As Van Gogh's brushstrokes
Flecks in the beard
Of a stranger posed
Solid and cool
A replica of David
Aloof in the fountain
Across from Cafe Toscano
Swept up in Colonia Roma
Through gilded mornings
Espressos and croissants
This unknown woman
Lost in her language
Luggage left behind
No name or address

Broadway, Manhattan

I remember reading Joe Brainard, a copy of his autopoetry
In the basement of The Strand inhaling dust and bookrot and
I Remember thinking about good titles being like a smile that says
Sex with a sibilant S

I was dawdling and meandering because there was nothing better
I had going on at that moment, a job easily performed intoxicated
An apartment by the steps up to the J/Z train in Bushwick

I remember women always, posh friends of my Cuban roommate
No panties over hair chevrons, miming Basic Instinct and drinking
Moet

I had no inkling why that was the trend in Manhattan for the few hot
Months of July and August, during the long humid hot-hot summer
Of 2011

I chafed a lot in the commuter heat of the G train, drinking spit warm
Rosé from a To Go cup straw, listening to the obese line cook, E, while
He talked out a ten-year jail sentence and six children with five
Women

I watched the Freedom Tower millimetering its erection way up
Through the swirl of gulls and occasionally dipping its tip in the
Cumulus

I slept on the roof, after fights with her that could've brought down
The sky, under the airborne highway to LaGuardia, night lit up like
A cineplex aisle

Knickerbocker Avenue, Bushwick

I scrunched up my nose at the fake butter flavor popcorn and
Scallop smell on the twilit blue beach at Coney Island as the sun
Petered out into waves

I tried to talk my way through, translating ingles a español and
Back into OVO Spanglish, Woody Allen's Manhattan projected
On an inflatable screen

We hid from the film crew, rebroadcasting us illegals back
To ourselves, making our real neighbors on blankets in the sand
Self-conscious

I turned and saw two waxed vaginas, pores like grit in bare toes
Skin blue as water the tide has yet to pull out, on a red and white
Gingham blanket

I laughed like a jet engine on the way home, there they were again
Nothing but nylon between them and the vibrating yellow plastic
Seats on the E train

I ran like a match on gasoline when I woke up on our roof
To eyes in the night leering through the fence that summer
My love hid out in daylight on the tarpaper and whitewashed
Our found furniture, her hands like chalk sculptures floating
Above Knickerbocker, screaming to the bleat of rap leaked from
Car windows sliding by so many stories below

Elegy for Network TV

Ever present this faceless, nameless
Everyday ambition strangling each
Me. I surrender on a Friday, cut
Off the sweet flow of oxygen and let
My eyes see stars in the darkness
Behind eyelids. Wake up on a
Clear Saturday with a hard-on
And a hangover, watch the others
Complain about banks and wealth
Disparity, while I eat my breakfast
Biscuits with gravy, regularly shit
Talk my feelings on Sunday before
A big flat screen, American football
Commentary blares. On wan Monday
Returns with a sorrowful, muted bray
Brings acid indigestion and discontent
A weekend of entertainment and decay

Kin

There is something so beautiful
In the lavish
      beating of your child
      with a painting   snapping
The spine
           of the frame across a brow reminiscent
Of your own
Imagining kin
      as replication
Of self
Indelible as fantasies
Put down
         in brush strokes of oil
A landscape gone or
Buried   a replacement
      bought online
Rehung
On the same wall
Mounted
From the same nail

Losing My Faith

Midweek, a fogless morning
I wandered alone, hungover
Again into a noodle house
On Broadway in San Francisco
Chinatown with an empty belly

But when the woman set down
A steaming bowl of pho and
I crushed fresh cut leaves
Of basil, a memory came
Flooding back into childhood

Reveries of hands in water
Submerged in a creek, green
Where we set sail to many ships
Of glued toothpicks and popsicle
Sticks licked clean but stained

You'll remember, another time over
A similar dragon dancing blue
On porcelain, we were still lovers
Seated across from each other
In a booth beside a window

Back in Toronto that memory too
Intertwined with basil and wide lips
Your eyes set on death falling divergent
Spreading malignantly upstairs in bed
Your father's sadness, beauty withered

2

Into too many words destroyed
By stutters and a lack of language
We drank struggle and danced out
Our worries with gallons of life
Red while leaves filled the gutters

Along windy Harbord Street coloured
Autumn racing through Canadian chill
Together on our bicycles, always your
Black coattails billowing out behind and
I keeping close, a silent eye on the road

Ahead, after the first snow white
Fell as we walked through glittering
Air frozen in sodium halos at Sturgeon
Point, drunk in your thighs clenched tight
My ears flaming with frostbite scars, absent

3

As your pleasure, at his funeral in February
I arrived unannounced and told you I loved
Your soul like an arrogant knife, but we were
Sharp and true those years, after we bumped
Into each other again, before I left for good

So that in the city of our youth and eternal
Crossing patterns, you I saw in my eyes no
More, on the way to study in Chicago, but
Now you drift back into my thoughts, like dragons'
Breath steaming in a bowl of pho here and now

And when the shitty radio starts to play
Losing My Religion, we dance blind again
One last time, you're thoughtlessly in my mind
Reassuring my faith in a god made up entirely
Of coincidence and concatenation like *Oh no*

I've said too much, I haven't said enough

Chicago-San Antonio, Texas Eagle

A prison like a ghost freighter
The man is looking silently
Out the window at a reflection
Unable to give his attention to any
One aspect of the beautiful woman's face
The night Train devours space along
The track, metal sculpts a glimmering edge
On the Mississippi with a blade of light
As fine and superficial as a single lash
She gasps and places a hand at her lips
His face becomes sullen and blank
As the dull white of a scrubbed hull
An edifice, magnificent as crystal shards
Of a chandelier seen through a flute
Spilling effervescent champagne down
Her throat, comes rising fast as a current
Tugging them apart and drawing their eyes
Into an endless cyclone fence of barbed wire

The Dakota Hotel, San Francisco

Imagine a faultless path aiming
Carelessly through green grass
Off the lip
Look back at the city from Sausalito
Hear the siren swing swoosh of a hardwood bat
Coming clean
Through the sultry air toward your teeth
A split pelt of blood and chipped enamel
Gnats like a mushroom cloud
Drift in
That crooked August
Heat
Rise in the wave
I want to be all
The feelings that have accrued
Pull off my shirt
       and let it blow over the edge
              of the roof at Taylor and Post
              on the sunburnt shoulders of Dante
Compare sunshine to egg yolk and the view from up here
Draped over your spine
Staring down boots at the concrete
Our eyes walk away
Through The Tenderloin
            and down to the bay

Walking

Walking briskly to the train stop
Walking quietly to the bathroom
In the night, walking a forest path
Walking carelessly along the side of a highway
Drunk, walking as if the world is spinning
Walking hand-in-hand with a lover
Walking down the aisle
Walking leisurely to the store for milk
In the morning, walking the walk
Of shame, walking with your hands cuffed
Behind your back, walking alone
Walking and talking and
Walking again
Walking after plaster is cut from the skin
Of your Achilles', walking like you won the lottery
On your first few steps of freedom
Walking with a limp in your calf when
Walking from house to car becomes
A fault line, walking through a parking lot
Lost, walking in circles and not
Walking with your silent steps

La Bodeguita Del Medio, D.F.

You're lying in bed smoking a joint
Cubano beats ushering in the noise
Chachacha from across the alleyway
When the first swarm lands on D. F.
Grasshoppers as long as gunships
Antennae like flagpoles reaching inside
Millions of open windows across the city
All of the reclined bodies awaiting a feeling
A breeze of ion-charged air, a pressure drop
Sit up and look and reach out your fingers
Locate the buzzing, your phone is ringing
Hear a lowercase love crying in a subdued tone
What's happening to this fucking shithole?
Whisper, It seems uncertain, while taking
A long steady pull of blue into your lungs
A breath held, more than humanly possible
Savour that extra little bit of latent potency
And exhale until everything black is true

Ubud, Bali

Water bottles perched on the windowsill
The morning roar of diesel engines
A sky like crumpled Marlborough foil
A girl, truly a woman, indecent and
So young her skin is still unchurned
Milk on the shadowed bedsheets

How they lay in a sodden sweaty mess
After a night of corkscrewing, dreaming
Of white worms the length of whales
Dipping their eternal eyes in and out
Of the milky way, consuming the stars

While you lay awake reciting Rimbaud
And smoking a whole pack of smokes
Lighting each anew with the molten
Cherry of the last as the filter singes
And sooty black crumples the edges

Of your memory, her forgotten name
The pocketed surface of volcanic rock
Beneath the carved face of Budha serene
And black, above the desk by the clock
Where two black hands circle until mist
Brings the rain across the rice paddies

Endless Cinema

From a collection, tangled and smooth
A hand reaches out as if to grasp or cup
Pry and struggle to gain hold, there is
Rubble strewn, crumbled as sandcastles
The director must have setup a wide shot
For effect, for calling out the thin-witted
Skeptical, gentle-kneed critics on IPhones
Who cannot bear a fictional catastrophe
Fractures have enveloped humanity's great
Constructs, museums and palaces, towers
Hawker stands and 7Elevens, all you rely on
Consumed by one tongueless mouth, silent
And it takes you a moment to realize the air
Muggy and sensual as a ghost lover's breath
Parakeet bruises color your body beautiful
Yet somehow you live, despite the physical

Siem Reap, Cambodia

My heart is beating slowly as a river
Rotten with centuries of sewage
Country music twangs along a dirt road
Not far from a Khmer kingdom rebuilt
After the burning red dogs attacked
Napalm kisses and metallic ticks buried
Wooden skeletons rotted from within
Laying dormant as caskets full of split
Atoms, neutrons and other fractions
Of an earth shattered and divulged
When mosquitoes land on my skin
Briefly I am alive with fire and gall
When the blood gently drains and I
Begin to incubate a million life forms
Each yet more intricate than my own
Sense of destiny and justice, like black
Sluice water dripping quietly into the ditch
I drop a cigarette and listen to the wet hiss
Briefly, a glimpse of my soul, broken and
Yet impregnable, everlasting as Angkor Wat

El Paso-Juarez, Tejas

The brevity of a scrawl
Taken quickly on a napkin
Like love and beauty
Immediately crumpled in a fist
Sweat-tinged and bloody
knuckles resting on a table
In a diner on the highway somewhere far out
But too close
Desert twilight, phosphorus magenta and lime
Shimmers briefly
Before the waiter can bring the bill
Her eye catches a glint of fluorescent
Tubes fluttering like extraterrestrial
Caskets, soggy dreams packed tightly as
Enchiladas Rojas half-eaten and forgotten
Through the porthole of a kitchen door
A scrawny teenager, unlit cigarette on his lip
A tattoo of the *Virgen de Guadalupe*
Scarring his chiseled forearm black, scrapes
Clean the remains of an unpalatable dinner
Left in the wake of her unspoken words
Stand up and wake from the earth
Open a faucet and dip your head in ice
Cold water, look at your face, false poet
Out of place and fractured
A silent drive atop a two-stroke engine
Under a deafening sidereal darkness

So heavy you imagine yourself, Atlas
Until the key clicks in the lock
And the door falls open to anywhere
Sepia sheets with hospital corners
The click of a lamp on a nightstand
The ruffle and swish as you undress
A painful scorching nakedness
Unfulfilled by a sleepless night
This body lying within your breath

Broken Meter

Watch red numbers spin
Endlessly circle the meter
Night flames on the small
Lips of a busker working
The streets of Distrito Federale
On a long sinuous ride to home
So frightfully far from your own
Mexico City, millions of beacons
On a starry sea of streetlights
Glimmering on putas' leggings
Cruising in ever widening gyres
The old city walls tilted off keel
Like a ghost Spanish gallion afloat
On the mellow waves of the gulf
Adrift in a youthful revolt, desire
Always returns you here, her home
Long black curls like a riptide
Eyes humid with concentric hate
Lips so stubborn and shallow they
Drown wrapped on a mezcal bottle
A note tossed overboard at four
In the morning, everything calm
As the nines roll up like blind eyes
And click back to cross-eyed zeros
Scroll through your list of contacts
Imagine a world your own, impossible
To be alone in a city of twenty million
And yet here you are in the backseat
Counting streetlights and empty blocks

Watching yourself from a white airplane
Window in a distant (no) remote (no) other
Time before you floundered into the foreign
Impossibility of love, half-expecting to be
Overcharged for a meter that lost count
Of the days and weeks and months and
Years since you've been able return home

Upstream

I dreamed of a shallow riverbed full
Of children's limbs, knotted and
Grappling like eels beneath rapids
Feet and fingers, the circular
Spume frothing gray as thunderheads
Rocky ledges and outcroppings blurred
Red, as I fell, like capillaries and veins
Earth stratified by aeon after aeon
Shouts and giggles echoing up and
Through my cavernous soul, I held back
My hands, clutched ribs and heartbeat
In an eternal embrace, whitecaps
Rose to meet my descent, furious
As the youthful agnostics below
Crushed by the empathy of their own
Weight, swimming fruitlessly upstream
Toward an ocean that will never arrive

Fish Sauce Sun

The poppies sag and drop
A trail of crimson on concrete
A pair of plain-Jane pigeons
Do their best hen impression

Out here in the west the sun comes
Right at you, up in your face light
Catches and shines on the tail pipe
Of a shit-brown Toyota pickup

You can't exactly describe how
This light differs from back home
But you know in your soul how
It hits you like triple cherries on slots

You've hit the fucking jackpot
With this one, it's a *bon mot* for
The ages, a little *je ne sais quoi*
Your Lucky brand fish sauce sun

Apollo Bay, Victoria

Watching the Milky Way move
Over an empty motel parking lot
Out along the Great Ocean Road
Cicadas chirring, the brilliant sound
Of the sea washing across the dark
Night, a loneliness like you've never
Known, somewhere between old age
And the terrible fiasco of trivial youth
Lost in the interminable middle of
Grace and fraudulence that you call
Hymn, a place where nothing resides

In The Cool of The Day

That black brown purple blue blood
Stain on his chest heaving wet
A white tee shirt marked forever by slipshod
Hands and a serrated knife, the smell
Of cordite, the long barrel and an eternity
As a doe stands in the cool of the day

Oven roasting like singe sick skin flesh
A fire inside seared lightly, discreet
Grill marks on the meat ruler straight black
As ash under the eyes, eye black shadowed
A man's man not mascara nor kohl, athlete
Trapped, a woman burst from his cranium, never
Been to Athens, nor read of Diana, cuts accordingly

A diagram tacked with rusty nails to a barn post
Heavy wet haysmell like sex, honey, Spring and olive
Sprigs, the parts of her body divided into territories
Analogies, Disney made easy, purple-hipped red hinds
Forelegs of cerulean blue, a big green blotch in the middle
Where her heart once beat, waiting with plates set for the drip

To slow, staunch the blood flow, floor thick crimson curled
Rivulets in the dust, Stygian rivers, estuaries growing like life
After death, we bow our heads and pray for our neighbours
On a wet slick window rattler, silver night like a blade reflected
Sickle moon comes into the kitchen and welcomes our hunger, lulls
Says, Sleep now, our father has provided, so let us rest our heads

Passages

Sometimes we drown in sweetness
And the hellfire of darting fox eyes
The wish quick whiplash of a hairy tail
Get drunk on the salted, fermented sweat
Dripping between shitty Converse sneakers
Lick the dotted borders of ingrown hairs
On the maps of our well-scarred ankles
Each time I swallow the harried
Anguish of your much too long looks
Burrowing through my eyes like a white
Grub, punch-drunk in a tossed bottle
Of Jalisco Tequila and the sorrowful drawl
Reflected in blue fields of agave
On the road south to Oaxaca, torrential
Downpours, colour explodes on the highway
A jackknifed fruit truck ripped down to the pith
Pavement stained every shade that red
Cannot describe in its monotonous tone
Wake up to an earthquake full of mezcal and
Forgotten jazz blowing stronger than memories
Stumble into a cathedral and fall on your bones
Feel hard soil waiting penitent with the infinite

El Raval, Barcelona

Her lips come rising above the alleyway, out of breath
A Greek in a flowing black dress smoking a bitchstick
Wrists draped in silken sweat, salted Mediterranean smile
On a terraza in Barrio Chino, keeping a journal in ink
Notes on thievery, Jean Genet, an Islamic barber
Whets his blade, children kick a ball against brick
The dull thud and whack, others scream from the slaps
Doled out by elders and siblings, sopping garbage men
Stroll home, still in uniform, as dusk grays on El Raval
Couples walk, sweaty palms clasped, drunks lean precariously
On plastic legs of patio chairs, smoke exhaled in cuneiform
Drifts over hundreds of white eyes gazing up at a depiction
In grayscale, violence on a whitewashed brick wall
There is nothing left now but her darkly painted mouth
A bed of embers, the white hot bulb behind a 16mm projection

Le Café Flo, Melbourne

Morning glides by on a bicycle
Seen over the blowing steam
Of a smooth flat white foaming
Beneath Saturday's upturned lips

A poodle tied to a post leans
Bodily weight against our table
We're a world away from home
Ourselves brought down under

For this little taste of nothing
A quietness complete despite
The sound of traffic and talk
Overheard from our neighbors

Nothing can bring us back
Across the oceanic divide
Separating happiness, calm
The startling truth of this life

Proteins

The slow kneading of your body
Rising under my hands, yeast
And something nameless here
Wafting in the air between our
Lips, hands gently folding back
Blade where my thumb finds
A niche, a spine like abandoned
Steel girders laying a track way
Out to infinity, out on the horizon
In the dismal future of endless
Possibilities, all the other realities
When the fields have gone to seed
And the oven has cooled, when our
Bodies no longer need this ferment

San Jose Del Pacifico, Oaxaca

There is a mountain that I climbed
Four hours south of Oaxaca after I woke
To an earthquake in an empty room
Legs shaking from a night of Mezcal
Walking in the rain
Alone on naked cobblestones
In the city washed clean
Of everything but the night
Drunk enough to let the water
Blur into light
Spilling from street vendors' carts
Searing pork fat
Silent cigarette smoke
The long ride, a strobe
Of cinder block houses
And military checkpoints
Nothing but
A few skinny teenagers
Kalashnikov rifles grinning
In their camouflage

2

Up the hill
I walked again
Past the supply store
Past the line of men, drunk
Enough to see their dead
Others floating in clouds
Past the public school
A child drove a flatbed truck
Brimming with earth
Pulled from the surface
Past the rusty orange Volkswagon campervan
The blue lick of hashish
Smoke flowed
Past Doña Maria's chimney
Up the last bend
With scrawny dogs in tow
Feet buried
To the ankles in earth

3

After I had seen what
I had searched for
I stripped myself bare
In the cabaña overlooking
Lesser peaks
A graveyard of green
Bodies rising
Under fingerling clouds
Held fire and tinfoil
Breathed
Heroin fumes until pressure squirmed
Beneath my skin
Dissolved into a fine mist of crawling
Ants and I
Watched the clouds burn over
Mountains' bosom
All the way to the ocean
A hundred and twenty kilometers
Disappeared from clarity
To fog and I
Swallowed
In a sallow-mouthed mist

4

Shivering at dusk
I became aware
Of his presence
Beside my own
His face
As pale as a reflection
Moonlight on a puddle in the mud
Washed out by rain yet
Clear enough to reveal
Eyes staring back at me
Air whistled from his lungs
And his body fell
Hard on his skull
Even then I tried to tell him
We were above a world
Apart
I know he heard my voice
Whispering into the clouds
Blowing through his darkness
Down the glistening drip of blood
Streaking his temple
Into a starry black sky
Only
The mountains listening
As his breaths climbed and
Hung

Orillia, Ontario

On the flat shores of Coouchiching
Where washed pebbles meet bitumen
Returned home to love lost, found
New joy in the sandy sweeps and

Green hills, green grass, green May
After the wave break of black traffic
On the 400 North from city blocks
This endless panoramic of square

Cut acreage, sown and fallow alike
Separated by narrow hues of ocher
Tepid yellows, lavender, gray, dark
Blues reflecting white cirrus, hollow

Cheeks and a sienna freckled bridge
Nose pink, lips mumblings of the artist
Over the verdant glass ripples, violet mist
Rising from this lake in a land of many

Kensington Market, Toronto

In the market, she walks down Augusta Avenue with
A Bosch pear and a swollen grapefruit, one in each
Hand and a subtle, lassitudinal sway to her hips
A face like my paternal grandmother, stern and British
Unleavened yet, her body seamless and wan with
The squareness of a child, anger and fierceness in her
Eyes, unintentionally sighted again, on a morning with
Rainstreaked windows and pearled condensation
Mana spotting the bins of produce like gems
A bin of laundry under her elbow and a ruddy
Apple missing a bite, her breasts free of a bra, again
An elusive and hypnotic sway in her confident stroll
Undefinable and strange, she must have uncanny timing
As her shopping bags bloom, verdant green roughage
Fringes a sharp, nubile gleam on her two eggplants

Prince Edward County

A turkey is roasting in the oven
We are laughing hysterically
In a cloud of cigarette smoke
The greasy pall of a wood stove

Empty bottles piled on the table
We've drank a whole skyline
Of red wine, whiskey and vodka
No one can remember who began

A throaty laugh like a full ballpark
Doing the wave in late October
Every decibel becomes a sacred oath
Purple lips and throats an invitation

This is the kind of party that lasts
A sponge alligator growing in the tub
Until it takes on Homeric proportions
Like stories whispered between stalls

Our hangovers will have middle names
They'll put new postal codes on the map
A silent girl will spew a legendary tsunami
Of Eggnog and rum across the potato salad

Hut The Hunting Dog will lead our troops
Into a white night like a flannel Carnivale
Leaping over tall hay bales in a single bound
Til suddenly earth wraps us all in a headlock

And a flurry of stars open up above us with the cool
Hiss of a King Can whispering in wordless prayer

Hunting Spiders

I want to bury you deep under
A layer of damp mulch and topsoil
I'd sniff you out like a truffle pig
Head down, nosing into underbrush

I want to bury you deep under
A downy felt of fresh white snow
I'll use my teeth to shovel you out
Tongue stuck as I lick ice from each

                             frozen window

I'd sniff you out like a wet ferret
Hunting spiders under a dank dock
I'll dig through floorboards in search
Of a nest for our stinky little flock

I'll use my teeth to shovel you out
A fertilizer black square flowerbed
I want to bury you in a tangle of red
Roses and thorns to prick your skin

Underwater

I find her lying down with her eyes

Closed, feet up on the gunwales of our
Bathtub, water blue as light beyond a reef
Her swollen sex gaping as a fish's mouth
A cigarette burned to the filter on the sink
Lavender-scented smoke from a stick of incense
Fills the moist air with a disconcerting note
I am yelling from an animal depth I've forgotten
Bubbles slip up between her thighs and hair
Comets are falling across the city like rapture
It's on all the channels, everyone is freaking out
Silence is a false promise, a meek deception
There aren't supposed to be any secrets in this
But I know I am always the last to know and
The serenity of floating says everything, all that

I could possibly ask with her eyes open

In The Womb

The backlash against making the world
Into a woman, seeing continents carved
Of breasts and succulent hips
The Cape of Good Hope
A calve carelessly turned inward
Sri Lanka, Ceylon, call it what you will
See a spot of sweat
Dripping from mother India's loins
But always only
See what is imagined
Not real cartographies, no more
Than a series of lines
Pretending to be square
When there is simply none
There in the knot of an oak
Find the clitoris bulging
Calling you into an embrace
Of sap and rough skin
Tracing up the steep hills
Of San Jose del Pacifico to the
Mountaintops of the Sierra Madres
Laid out along the ridge of her spine

No number of kilometres is enough
To describe the effulgent flow
Of her back and sweet cradle of green
Breasts rising and falling
Towards that infinite tide that lulls
Softly on the beach, salty vaginal sea
Opening each morning and receding
With the sliver of moon, the crease
In the armpit of the night sky
Stamped by shamelessly beautiful spots
Running down her bending body
You will always see this and more
The wave curling her hair, glowing
White in a starlit senescent touch
And to be content is to know
That you will bury the body inside
Of this tomb that is earth, or better yet
You will fall one day from the cliffs
On the precipice of her shoulder blades
Leap into her waters and drown
In the unending bliss of her deep
And incubating womb

Deep Sea

Green digits on the oven clock
Rosemary, butter and sea salt
Sizzle and crackle of crisp skin
A whole bird
Roasting on a nest of baby
Yukon Gold potatoes, split and boiled
A sound like a bird chirp
The friction of your ass cheeks
As your back arches above linoleum
It's still too early, I don't
Want to come up
For air, my eyes are closed
Diving into a paradise of salt
Water, snorkeling inches
Above sharp edges of coral
Reef, shoals of tiny metallic fish
Dart in and out, the snub-nosed tip
Of an eel peeking from the dark
Shadows in the fissures, weightless
And free to explore, sea turtles cruise
Through my vision, thousands of soft
Mouths all lightly nibbling, gingerly
Tickling along the living fingers
Of an underwater ecosystem, that sound
Of a million underwater kisses
All at once, brings us rushing
Back to the surface, each
Breath gasping for air

On a Jet Plane

I'm stuck in flight
Somewhere over
An ocean just like you
Lost everywhere
Between thirty thousand feet and
An airline magazine
Stolen and stuffed
Into your carry-on, my whole
Jealousy seems mundane
From this height it's just
Me and you, baby, so
Crazy I think I love you
Long time, same same
But different your
Cliché is my front door
Give love a try maybe
You and me together
Stars and stripes forever
Stuck in the middle of
You, true blue baby, say
Baby and maybe just maybe
Your dream will come true
Before we touch down

San Miguel, Guanajuato

The sprawling parking lot
Of a grocery superstore
Bent right from Ginsberg's
Stanzas and pesadillas
I'm having a literary
Moment, standing behind
A pickup truck with a cage
Inside there's a tiger
Circling, striped with conviction
Dreamt and paradoxical yet
Real enough that the kids stop
And stare, ice cream cones held
At right angles, paused before
Open lips and slack jaws, I am
Comparing this orange slave
To Borges' liquid dreams, a mind
Fuck, it is so much bigger than I
Could imagine, breaths that rumble
Eyes that pierce with clarity, knowledge

Of its interminable predicament, a circus
Cat, I was visiting Niall Cassady's grave
An unmarked spot on the railway
Tracks just past San Miguel Allende
Bent out of shape like Bukowski
Someone asked why there wasn't more
A marker or a cross, a chicken clucking
A potbelly child staring through a fence
And the rails began to vibrate beneath
Our feet, warning of an impending arrival
Seen on our walk back to town, a big
Top and carnival packed down, tucked
Behind the station coloured with graffiti
And windowed with two-by-fours, I am
Lost in the words of this other tiger, stuck
In the quagmire of description, trapped
In the memory of a reference half-
Forgotten, spinning in an empty spot
Of this cárcel's sprawling parking lot

Snow

Drifting along the expressway
A Pontiac Voyageur glides on
A film of black and white
Powder tracing swirling lines
A slow dance down the off-ramp
Gullies harness drifts and accrue
Tiny accidents piled like shards
Beneath skyscrapers of glass
Fishscale fenestration flickers
With each white flake which falls
Holier than god, pockets of cloud
Whisper words for the homeless
Sewer grates' steel grins exhale
Soft breaths of warm air hissed
From the glinting iron behemoths
Snaking beneath the city's sewers
A perfect evening for a walk alone
Down the middle of dusted alleys
Streetlights shimmering radial glow
Rays of silver reaching into night
Sidereal harmony and footfalls
Each aspect quiet, becoming a city
Toronto under fresh fallen snow

At This Hour

It's not yet six in the morning
And only the cat, Patichou, and I
Preside over this slow blue dawn
The row of halfway houses sits quiet
Dipped in cream cheese clouds
The static television and neighbours
Savouring sleep before the cries of
Their toddlers scare off the spring
Magpies that never tire of taunting
Worms, at this hour it is just
The two of us, the winter hares
Gone silently into their burrows
To hump the day away, we can
Sip a coffee with the first caws
Listen carefully and hear the buds
Stretching off the tips of branches
And the river that still churns beneath
The city, before the first engine cuts
Into our thoughts and work begins

Whitefish, Montana

Everywhere you look it glitters
Afternoon sky lit up with white
Puffs of cotton seed pods drift
In through the open window

On the breezeway of southern
Transit, all these enunciations
Of trees still unimaginable in
The way their roots will spread

I am in love with this exact
Iteration of June, its golden
Delight on forearms, subtle
Flutter of electricity dancing

Quiet between our fingertips

Whitmanesque

Oh man, Oh death, what love we have
For the stars, every memory of Hollywood
All the marketplace push and pull, rise and
Rise up, the strenuous folly of future tense
The present, so full of itself, all a twitter
The songbirds are dying, a plague upon
Our land, much greater than a nation state
Of affairs, tremulous and withering, what will
We take on the final walk to the bridge, cross
Over to Brooklyn, to Prague, to Busan and back
To the levee break, let it all wash away, songs
Old and new as identity, only creation untamed
Exists

. . .

Acknowledgments

The author, Evan A. Jordan, offers his profuse thanks to all of the people that helped him develop, edit, revise and polish the poems in this collection.

He would not be a writer if it weren't for many incredible teachers and mentors: George Elliot Clarke, Sharon English, David Gilmour, David Layton, Sylvia Legris, A.F. Moritz and M.G. Vassanji were all inspiring, helpful and supportive during his years at the University of Toronto and The Humber School for Writers. Thanks are due as well to the editors of Matrix Magazine, CV2, The Antigonish Review, Acta Victoriana, Arc Magazine and Pank, all of whom encouraged or published parts of this collection over the years. Also, many thanks to the people at Wattpad HQ, for big ups and bucks and that little bump. A special thanks to Zoe and Caitlin!

To friends and Family, as well, infinite thanks: Adia, Ceci, Dougal, Eric, Faye, Frank, Jason, Jer, Julia, Kyrsten, Linds, Matt, Mina, Nane, Nick, Noah, Paul, Rosie, Sean and Sharon. Thanks for sifting through the trash bin and helping to decide what was worth recycling.

Many of these poems were written during my years on Sangre de Cristo y es necesario que di gracias a la gente de Cafe Tal y Cafe Antik. A todos que me ayudaron y al papa quien mató todas las palomas de las calles de Guanajuato, gracias!

About The Author

Evan A. Jordan currently teaches language and creativity classes and workshops. He is a Wattpad Star and the author of two serial novels (*SURV13VORS, Winnower*), a collection of stories (*Didn't I Tell You?*) and a work of non-fiction (*365: The Creative Planner*).

He has has been a Script Consultant, Editor, Slush Pile Reader and 21st Century Nomad. Born in Toronto, he has lived in Vancouver, San Francisco, Mexico City, Brooklyn and Melbourne. Find him at:

Evanajordan.com
Twitter.com/evanajordan
Instagram.com/evanajordan

Photo credit: jasonmortlock.com

CPSIA information can be obtained
at www.ICGtesting.com
Printed in the USA
LVOW11s0053200417

531463LV00003B/376/P

9 781366 327062